In Memoriam

This book is dedicated to the memory of my parents
Owen Allen (1922-2003)
Ethel Allen (1924-2006)

contents

The Obverses:

contents

The Reverses:

Britannia

George & Dragon

Lion & Crown

Rose Florins

Shields:

i) Conventional

contents

Shields:

i) Conventional (continued)

ii) Cruciform Shields

iii) Triple Shields

Wreaths

Miscellaneous

introduction

There is no subject in the coin world more controversial than that of grading. Even well-established dealers vary slightly in their assessment of how a coin should grade, and as for coins sold over the internet, I have seen pieces for sale which I would class as being a full two grades out (e.g. a 'fine' coin being described as 'extremely fine'). I felt therefore, that there was room in the market for a pictorial guide to help collectors grade the most common coins currently collected in the UK – i.e. British coins produced from 1797 to the end of the pre-decimal series, usually taken as 1970.

So to start from basics, the following is the description of the main states of condition which affect milled circulation currency* (and this book is mainly concerned with circulation coins) taken from the companion volume to this, 'Collector's Coins Great Britain':

UNC: *Uncirculated:* Like the name suggests, the coin should be as it left the mint with no signs of circulation or wear. Not necessarily perfect though, because coins can pick up scratches and what are known as 'bag marks' during mass production and contact with other coins at the mint. The coin should have most of its lustre present and some dealers may expect 100% lustre on coins stated as Uncirculated.

EF: *Extremely Fine*: A coin with little sign of being circulated. There may be only the slightest wear to the highest areas and minimal scratches and other marks. Often some of the mint lustre is visible on coins of this grade. As a rough idea a coin in your change would probably be an EF if it had been lucky and was minted just 1 year ago.

VF: *Very Fine*. A coin with some wear to the highest areas of the design but which has seen limited circulation. More hair detail is evident and also detail on the other designs. Just as an average guide a coin that has been in normal circulation for approximately 5 years may qualify for VF status.

F: *Fine*. Fine coins show considerable wear to all raised surfaces. Some detail should be visible on the designs and some of the main hair volume should be visible on the Monarch's head. Not individual strands, but maybe a parting or signs of head-dress. Many of the coins in your pocket even after just 30 years or less of normal use would probably be Fine or less.

*You will however see the occasional reference to coins in FDC, a condition which applies only to proof specimens. FDC stands for fleur-de-coin and means absolutely perfect in every way, without wear, scratches or hairlines etc.

Fair: Heavily worn, but with readable legend and major points of design identifiable. It would be reasonable to say that the vast bulk of 20th century coins in this condition are worth no more than their metal value.

Poor: These are not just smooth disks but actually identifiable coins. However, the list of shortcomings can be extensive, ranging from a few letters obliterated in the legend, to coins in which virtually the only detail visible is the date. A very few coins will still retain a value over and above the metal content, but they would need to be pretty rare.

These are good clear descriptions which give the reader an idea of how a coin should be graded. Nonetheless, 'a picture is worth a thousand words' and many observers have commented that the coin world has long been in need of a fully illustrated guide to grading British coins. Following discussions between myself and Chris Perkins on the www.predecimal.com forum, I offered to start work on a pictorial grading guide and this book is the result.

However, to return to the mechanics of grading, the coin community refines these descriptions by appending the basic terms with the words 'good' or 'almost' (sometimes interpreted as 'about' or even occasionally 'nearly') to describe coins better or worse than the stated grade e.g. Good Very Fine, Almost Fine etc. This can be a little confusing as some numismatists, principally but not exclusively in America, tend to use the term 'Good' and 'Very Good' in place of the British 'fair'.

Now, as well as a love of coins, I would confess to a love of the English language and it is my personal view, that any grading term which runs counter to the accepted meaning of words should be discouraged, hence even if 'fair' often overstates the case, I prefer it to variations on 'good' which in numismatic terms means pretty much the opposite of its accepted definition. To go to ridiculous extremes, you will see that technically the term *Good Good* is theoretically possible even if it isn't a particularly good coin.

As a general rule, I believe *'nearly'* to be a more honest term than *'about'* which simply serves to sugar the pill that a coin *isn't quite* the stated grade. The accepted definition of the word *'about'* is 'approximately', or 'more or less' and always carries a degree of uncertainty. As such its use in a numismatic context is capable of causing all sorts of linguistic confusion ('What grade is that coin?' 'Oh, it's about very fine,' 'Do you mean about very fine or *about* very fine…?'). I would concede however that the *uncirculated* grade can reasonably be prefixed with 'about' , if only for the reason that it makes no sense whatever in common parlance, and therefore the chances of confusion are lessened. Undoubtedly however, the most logical way of describing coins which fall between grades is by the use of the symbols '+' and '-'. Although this is used by some dealers, the industry in general has been slow to adopt what is only common sense.

The word 'uncirculated' itself carries some controversy, when what is actually meant in most instances is 'appears to be uncirculated'. If we are being honest, the only coins which should technically fall into this category are those where this can be proven i.e. still sealed in mint rolls etc. Everything else has been handed over by a bank cashier to somebody on the other side of the little glass screen, and is therefore *circulated*. Some dealers agree, for example Michael Gouby has pioneered the use of the initials PAS (Practically As Struck) for non-proof coins in the highest grade, which, whilst giving an accurate description of a coin does not tell a potential untruth. From a personal perspective, whilst I accept that its use is not intended to defraud, I would like to see the industry move away from a term which ultimately does it no credit. However, it is now so ingrained within the hobby that it may be a tad unrealistic to expect it to disappear in the short, or even the long term.

A welcome recent development in the UK market concerns the grading of high quality base metal coins where it is increasingly becoming the practice to quote the amount of lustre a coin carries as a percentage of that coin's surface. This makes sense from a commercial point of view where a coin in AU with 85% lustre can be worth two or three times as much as a coin in similar condition on which the lustre has all but disappeared. The percentage can be quoted either as a whole or one surface at a time. It sits alongside but does not affect the actual grade e.g. GEF20/15 which means a coin in Good Extremely Fine condition with 20% lustre on the obverse and 15% on the reverse. This is a considerable advance on the old practice of putting B (for 'brilliant') in front of the grade – usually 'uncirculated' to denote a high, but undefined percentage of lustre.

The Sheldon Scale – An Alternative View

This is a system first used in 1949 by Dr. William H. Sheldon in his book 'Early American Cents' where a numerical scale replaces the traditional system. Oddly, the highest numeral used is 70, which translates as perfection, but business (i.e. non-proof) strikes seldom grade above 65. Although not often used in the UK, it certainly has the advantage of avoiding all the semantic problems I have highlighted above. The only real criticism I can find to level at this system is that it introduces a secret code which is entirely impenetrable to non-collectors, and reinforces the stereotype of coin collectors as being fully paid up members of the anorak fraternity. Anyway, the Sheldon scale with comparison to both UK and Traditional U.S. grading is shown on the next page.

The legendary Gothic Crown in **GEF** condition.

UK Grading	Traditional US	Sheldon Scale	Additional ANA[1]
	Poor	PO1	
Poor	Fair	FR2	
	Almost Good	AG3	
Fair	Good	G4[2]	
Almost Fine	Very Good	VG8[2]	
Fine	Fine	F12[2]	
Good Fine	Very Fine	VF20[2]	
Very Fine	Very Fine	VF30[2]	Choice
Good Very Fine			
	Extremely Fine	EF45	Choice
Nearly EF			
Extremely Fine	About UNC	AU50[2]	
Good EF	About UNC	AU55	Choice
	About UNC	AU58	Very Choice
About UNC	Uncirculated	MS/PR60[2]	Poor
About UNC	Uncirculated	MS/PR61	Unattractive
About UNC	Uncirculated	MS/PR62	Acceptable[3]
Uncirculated	Uncirculated	MS/PR63[2]	Rather Attractive
Uncirculated	Uncirculated	MS/PR64	Quite Attractive
Uncirculated	Uncirculated	MS/PR65	Very Pleasing
Uncirculated	Uncirculated	MS/PR66	Above Average
Uncirculated	Uncirculated	MS/PR67	Exceptional
Uncirculated	Uncirculated	MS/PR68	Exceptional
Uncirculated	Uncirculated	MS/PR69	Exceptional
FDC	Uncirculated	MS/PR70	Perfect

[1] American Numismatic Association additional designation.

[2] These are the standard benchmark grades set out in the best known American price guide (The Official Red Book by R.S. Yeoman and Kenneth Bressett, published by Whitman Publishing Company LLC).

[3] Or 'Low Appeal' in the case of proof coins.

With a little thought, it is possible to work out what the lettering next to the numeral means, but those not encountered so far are:

MS = Mint State

PR = Proof

using this book

I would first of all like to stress that this is a *guide* and not a *bible* and the pictures themselves are not definitive i.e. to fit in to a certain grade, a coin need not look exactly like the example depicted; coin wear is far too random for that. All I am providing is no more and no less than pictures of coins of a similar design in a range of conditions, which may or may not look like your own example. The more coins wear, the less uniform they become; for example, the set of coins marked; 'Queen Victoria Bun Head, Fine condition' is likely to be far more variable than 'Queen Victoria Bun Head EF condition'. What you should be able to do however, is to compare your coin with the picture and calculate whether the amount of wear it has is approximately similar to the coin marked EF, VF, F or Fair, or indeed if, using the detailed pictures of most likely wear points, it is better than EF and is perhaps AU.

Furthermore, it must be remembered that the examples given for each grade are simply my opinion of a coin *in that grade*. A very large number of perfectly acceptable coins had to be rejected because in my view their grade needed to be prefixed with the words 'good' or 'nearly'. I had considered including examples of such 'fractional grades' in the book, but not only would this have made the logistics of tracking down so many coins extremely difficult, but the final result would have approached the size of a telephone directory! On the other hand, although coins in fractional grades have been excluded, there is still some latitude within the actual grades themselves, and so some coins are at the top of their grade, some are at the bottom, whilst others are dead in the middle. This is just the way of the world, and it would have been a Herculean task to track down more than three hundred images all of which sat primly in the middle of their grade. With succeeding editions, it will no doubt be possible to gradually exclude coins which are slightly to one side or the other, but for the time being it has been a big enough task to amass sufficient satisfactory photographs to go to press with all bases adequately covered.

Logically, one set of obverse pictures has been used for a whole range of coins from farthing to sovereign where that portrait is common to all. It would have been a long and tedious book were this not so. Similarly, where a range of obverses has been paired with a common reverse, these too have been merged into one section.

What should be borne in mind however, is that smaller coins generally start off with less detail. For example, in a fully struck up example of an 1839-47 crown in the highest condition, there should be sufficient detail in each of the six lions to identify what looks like a face. However, some 1887 sixpences also carry the six lions, but the best you are likely to get in a small coin intended for circulation is the face forming a kind of tiny dome, with little or no detail.

One or two very scarce designs have been omitted, as obtaining satisfactory images in a range of grades would have been extremely time-consuming, and would undoubtedly have delayed publication of the book. Similarly, designs which are seldom seen in a range of grades, e.g. the reverse of the Churchill crown, have also been left out, as nothing would have been gained by their inclusion. In fact the only use I have had for the poor Churchill is for the illustration of 'bag abrasions'!

And why 1797? This was the first year that coins were produced by anything like automated methods, and therefore defined the beginning of modern British coinage. This did throw up a few questions as to what coins should be included between that date and the great re-coinage of 1816. Despite their curious history, Bank of England Dollars were produced by Matthew Boulton at his Soho mint to much the same standard as the 1797 cartwheel coinage, and therefore had to be mentioned; if they were covered, then the Bank of England tokens of 1811-16 also demanded inclusion. In fact, the only coins I *have* omitted were the gold pieces – the guinea and its fractions - which were very much a part of the old order, and would not have sat comfortably with the other coins included herein.

At the other end of the line, post-decimal coins are dated from 1968, and thus overlap our period by some two years. Once again, these really belong elsewhere and have likewise been excluded.

It is almost inevitable that nobody is going to agree with 100% of the gradings in this book – that is just a fact of life, and whilst I hope that a majority of readers do not disagree too violently with my assessments, I may have to settle for an even split between those who think my grading is too harsh and those who feel it is too lax.

grading – some further points

There is quite a difference in the appearance of copper/bronze and silver/gold coins which spills over into the grading arena. A bronze coin in EF condition may be quite heavily toned, and what is more, any area of wear will probably be obvious by its different colouring. This does not mean that the underlying coin is necessarily in worse condition, just that it gives its grade away far more readily. With a silver coin, the collector is often faced with, if not hours, at least minutes with a magnifying glass to ascertain the same information that the bronze coin gave for free.

******

It is fair to say that the more recent the coin, the more stringent is the grading. For example, many of the coins illustrated as 'fair' in the George V third coinage (1927-36) would quite easily have passed for 'fine' had they been minted a hundred years before. I know that it is inconsistent, but that is simply the way that grading has developed, and who are we to argue – perhaps collectors have been too impatient for the coins to really attain a lower grade, if only to enhance the 'prestige' of those they already own, however slightly this may be. There are limits however, and I don't believe many Elizabeth II reverses from our era ever reached an overall 'fair' (although some more poorly struck examples of the first coinage obverse may come perilously close).

******

To check whether you are doing it right, look at the grades you have given to the coins in your collection. Is every third coin (or at least every third surface) in a 'whole' grade i.e. Fine, Very Fine, Extremely Fine etc? Or are there a disproportionate number of Almosts, Abouts, Goods, Maybes? It is simply human nature to avoid positive decisions, but try to get yourself into the habit of giving whole grades where at all possible. If you have a coin collection numbering say 300 coins, go through them all and try to fit the most appropriate 100 into whole grades. It is likely that you now have a more accurately graded collection than before.

grading — some further points

Lower grades tend to cover a much wider range of wear than their counterparts further up the grading scale. A coin in Extremely Fine condition will almost certainly have been in circulation for less than two years, whereas a coin in Fair condition could have seen anything from 20 to 50 or more years of circulation and so long as the design is discernable and the legend readable, the coin can still qualify as Fair. Another point about Fair condition is that whilst the legend has to be readable, small parts of individual letters can be worn away, just so long as they can still be recognised.

******

It is easy to forget that the teeth or beads around the rim form part of a coin's design and should be graded along with its more obvious points. A quick flick through this book will show that a coin in 'fine' condition is likely to have worn to the extent that the teeth will have merged with the rim in such a way that they are no longer distinct entities. Similarly, a coin one grade lower in 'fair' may well have lost both beading and rim altogether on at least a portion of the surface.

******

Grading coins above GEF is especially difficult. Due to handling when new and their conditions of storage, even high quality coins can tend to show some discolouration on the most exposed points, but this cannot be construed as wear, which manifests itself as a flattening of the metal. For the serious collector, a good magnifying glass is a must.

grading – some further points

At the top end of the scale, coins with no circulation damage are divided into two broad headings; 'About Uncirculated (AU)' and 'Uncirculated (Unc.)' (but see above regarding 'Practically as Struck'). It is very difficult to know where to draw the line, and it would be wishful thinking to believe that any yardstick was applied consistently. In general however, coins in AU may suffer from a number of defects such as excessive bag marks, being weakly struck or a total/partial loss of lustre. From my point of view (and bear in mind my previous comments on the Uncirculated grade), coins in truly uncirculated condition should have good eye appeal and in the case of copper/bronze coins, virtually all their mint lustre remaining. There are certain exceptions to this latter point e.g. most 1897-1917 farthings and pennies produced in the years 1934, 1935 (some) and 1944-46 which were toned by the mint. The definition of uncirculated is not quite as stringent with silver/silver coloured coins as toning is considered by many to be positively desirable. Again however, eye appeal is all.

To differentiate between the excellent and the stratospheric, dealers employ a number of superlatives; 'choice' is one frequently used, as is 'gem'. In fact anything that differentiates the top-notch (you could use that too!) from the workaday. I have even seen the word 'stonking' applied to a particularly notable example. At this level therefore, there are no rules and in all honestly, why should there be? More staid dealers, even in the UK, often fall back on the Sheldon Scale for their very best coins, but am I alone in thinking that this is something of a cop-out and a bit of honest over-hyping of a very good product just adds to the spice of life?

******

Although grading is the main determinant of a coin's price, we would be falling into Oscar Wilde's definition of the cynic ('A man who knows the price of everything and the value of nothing') if we did not acknowledge that attractive coins can occur right the way down the grading scale. Most of us start by collecting coins in lower grades, and we learn to discard those with patchy tone or a blob of some unspeakable substance on the reverse and replace them with more attractive coins, possibly in the same grade. Turn to page 114 and look at the 1871 penny listed as 'fair'; you will see its obverse on page 73. Although not grading highly, this coin is flat, round, has a good tone and no damage to speak of; I actually rather like it. Moreover, for the romantic, a well-circulated coin is far more evocative (think of who may have handled it…) than one which has seldom seen the light of day. I think what I am trying to say is that we are in the main collectors, not investors, and although a coin in a lowly grade may not be a great investment, it might nonetheless have its attractions. What is more it will cost a fraction of a coin further up the grading scale. If you like it, go for it, regardless of grade.

non-grading damage

These are just some of the misfortunes which can befall a coin without affecting its grade. If however I were buying a coin, sight unseen, I would feel pretty miffed if any of these were not mentioned:

Edge Knocks/Bruises – self explanatory. Being heavier, larger coins are more prone to such damage which can dramatically reduce their desirability and hence their value.

Cleaning – can be anything from being lightly immersed in Silver Dip (a proprietary solution which chemically removes the tarnishing from silver) to a full scale attack with Duraglit or some kind of rubbing compound. The latter will definitely send the coin's value into oblivion but it is a moot point whether dipping will. Generally speaking, dipping is tacitly accepted in America but treated with suspicion in the UK. For coins which have been more aggressively cleaned, look out for a mass of tiny lines in the field and an unusually 'metallic' appearance.

For base metal coins, cleaning should be obvious. Once the patina has been removed, it is nigh on impossible to get it back again in the same form; this does not however prevent people from trying…

Scratches – the older the scratch the better. Anything picked up in circulation and toned in with the rest of the coin may not have too great an effect on the value, depending of course on the quality of the rest of the coin. However, a recent scratch which reveals the shiny metal underneath could dramatically hit the value of a piece. A further point to take into account is whether the scratch was apparently accidental or patently deliberate, the former tolerated far more than the latter.

Graffiti – although closely related to scratching, the treatment of such coins could be rather different. It is not unusual to find pieces from the earlier part of our period and before, engraved with a name or initials; in fact this became an art form in its own right and many coins were carefully appended with the name of a sweetheart, usually in conjunction with that of the sender (presumably an apprentice engraver) and a short message. In extreme cases the entire coin was re-cut to a completely different design. The value depends on the quality of the engraving, but as historical documents these 'love tokens' are priceless.

Corrosion – gold is rarely affected by corrosion and although silver is not entirely immune, it is more likely to be seen in copper and its alloys – the dreaded verdigris (a kind of green deposit on the surface). Frankly, such coins should be treated with extreme caution. An ancient Roman coin displaying a little verdigris may be tolerated, a 1936 penny found on Littlehampton beach and covered in the stuff should be confined to the dustbin.

Some coins which were sent to the colonies when new, particularly those subjected to long sea journeys, tend to suffer from pitting to the surface. This does of course affect the value but it is difficult to obtain some dates/types (1827 penny, William IV half farthing) without it. Therefore even though afflicted in this way, such coins can still change hands for quite substantial sums.

Bag Abrasions – In some respects self-explanatory, but there is debate about what constitutes a bag abrasion, and how many a coin is permitted to have. Firstly, only coins in the highest grades are involved. Coins which are intended for circulation are produced in colossal numbers, which means that the mint can hardly treat them with kid gloves. They tumble out of machinery in great cascades, bouncing off their fellows and the sides of their containers. The coins are still technically uncirculated but have already accumulated a degree of damage. This is one of the points at which the grading system becomes a little illogical – does it matter whether the damage occurs at the mint or in the purse of the housewife, and how can we tell the difference? The answer is that quite simply, we just have to guess.

There are some pointers though; bag abrasions in their truest form should be a series of small scratches or knocks, and not the full scale erosion that would show up on the higher points of coins as a result of countless short-range collisions with their environment. Nonetheless, it would not be unknown for a coin to be downgraded to AU, GEF or even EF as a result of too much pre-circulation damage.

Not a terribly satisfactory state of affairs I know, but if we insist on calling coins 'uncirculated', rather than using some more logical assessment of their qualities, then bag abrasions will frequently be the subject of dispute.

Metal Flaws – usually small irregular holes on the surface of a coin, caused by air bubbles in the metal. They do have an affect on values, but how much would obviously depend on their size and whether they are in a prominent position on the coin.

Uneven Metal Mix – occurs in alloyed coins such as bronze. Usually shows up by variegated (usually streaky) toning and areas on the surface which do not tone at all. Has some, but in most cases not a huge, affect on value.

Carbon Spots - this is an affliction of high quality copper and bronze manifesting itself in tiny dark spots on the otherwise lustrous surface of a coin. Several theories have been put forward as to their origin, one of the most compelling being that they result from tiny drops of saliva landing on a coin following an injudicious sneeze in its vicinity. For this reason alone, coin collectors should always have a box of Kleenex handy…

Weak Strike – when assessing a coin, it is easy to downgrade it by assuming that all flattening of high points is due to wear. Many coins in point of fact were actually never struck properly at the mint, probably due to inadequate pressure being applied to the die, or where the die was itself excessively worn, and guess where this shows up most? Yep, in the places that would have worn first on a normal coin!

How these are graded depends largely on the grade they would otherwise have fallen into. If they have lots of lustre and appear otherwise uncirculated, you have every reason to describe them as such. If however you prefer to describe your best coins as 'Practically as Struck', then this is also true. On the other hand, if you were buying such a coin, you would have every right to feel aggrieved if the vendor had not appended the simple phrase, 'weak strike' or alluded to its shortcomings in some other way.

Where on the other hand, the coin was weakly struck and continued in circulation, then it is normal practice to grade it simply on what the observer sees. This does however lead to bizarre bi-grades such as F/EF, but at least the coin is being honestly described.

Typical bag abrasions on a Churchill crown

Pitting on an 1837 half-farthing

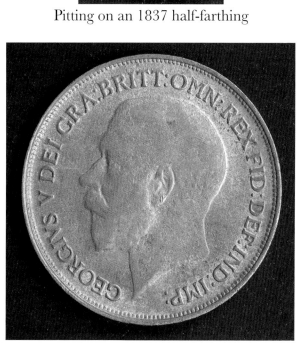

Weakly struck head on an otherwise EF 1918 penny

These (i.e. where one side of a coin is a different grade to the other) seem to occur in three different ways:

The use of a worn die – on one side or the other will result in the affected face appearing to show more wear than its counterpart. As time goes by, the cause will be less and less obvious but if it is assessed correctly, the grade may well always be lower on the affected side.

Coin is not flat – This happens more frequently than is generally realised and is often the result of a design fault. I have a 1902 King Edward VII crown in my collection which grades VF/NEF. When placed on a table with the reverse side down, it sits completely flat. Turn it over however, and it rocks on the pivot of the king's head which sits proud of the rim. The result of this is that the area of beard just below the ear (which is evidently the highest point) has worn more rapidly than anywhere else. I have not performed a survey, but it seems likely that this peculiarity will afflict all 1902 crowns, and hence many will be bi-grades.

The design on one side is bolder than the other – Take the obverse designs of Benedetto Pistrucci for Georges III and IV. Because of the large, heavy portraits and deeply cut lines, these often appear to wear less than whatever design occupies the reverse.

I did say three didn't I? Actually, why a coin wears more on one side is sometimes not obvious, but without one or other of the causes above coming into play, the difference is usually marginal.

Coins in 'Poor' Condition

Technically any coin on which the legend is no longer readable falls into this category. Although no serious collector would choose to collect coins this far down the grading scale, sometimes 'needs must' and 'poor' coins are used to fill gaps in a sequence of dates. As these are likely to be the scarcest years, it would be unreasonable to suggest that they have no value even though prices are never published.

Frequently, coins which have only just slipped off the bottom of the scale are described in such terms as 'legend weak obverse right hand side, otherwise Fair' or more prosaically 'Fair?'. With commendable chutzpah, the coin community has termed the very worst coins traded as 'clear date', the inference being that that is their only redeeming feature. Nonetheless, a search of the internet will often reveal 1863 farthings, 1871 halfpennies and 1869 and 1871 pennies all described as 'clear date' and offered for a few pence to a few pounds each.

Because of the protection afforded by a combination of rim and exergue line, the most likely coins to fall into the 'clear date' category are the 1860-95 bronze series, examples of which can frequently be little more than dated disks. The fact that such items are worth anything at all is testament to the health of the coin market and the wide range of income brackets that have been captivated by this fascinating hobby.

Poor   Poor

Poor (but see text)   Clear Date

section one
THE OBVERSES

Penny, Twopence

This was a seminal issue being produced to a very high standard at Matthew Boulton's Soho Mint; his concept being that the higher the quality of the coin, the less was the chance of convincing forgery, and in this he largely succeeded. Looking at the coins today however, the overwhelming impression is how large and unwieldly they are, but it must be remembered that they were produced at a time when the public demanded that any coin contain its full value of metal.

From a grading point of view, they are slightly unusual in having an extremely thick rim which to some extent protects the design, but is also prone to all sorts of knocks and sundry damage. It would be comparatively rare to find a lower grade specimen that didn't display a slightly frilled edge as evidence of its hard life. The twopences (which differed in having a proportionately larger head) left circulation comparatively early but many of the pennies remained in use up to and beyond the introduction of the new bronze coinage in 1860, finally being demonetised in 1869. The trouser pockets of Britain breathed a sigh of relief...

GEF. Beginning to show signs of wear on outer edges of laurel leaves; berries becoming very slightly flattened. Even in this grade, the coin is beginning to show signs of the damage which afflicts these heavy pieces.

EF

The easiest place to look for any wear is the outer edges of the laurel leaves and the nearby berries which may show wear by the slightest amount of flattening.

VF

Wear will now be obvious in most of the higher points, especially the hair over the ears, the ear lobe, the eye brow and the nose.

F

Most of the details are still clear i.e. the laurel wreath is still visible in its entirety, as are the ribbons and the major folds of the toga. The legend is still present in full.

Fair

Very little detail left on the portrait. The upper parts of most of the letters have been worn away.

Halfpenny, Farthing

Slightly less copper per unit of value than the cartwheel pennies and twopences, these are still very heavy coins. Without the massive rim of Matthew Boulton's earlier series, they are far more modern in appearance and judging by the condition of most examples, lived a hard life right up to the mid-Victorian period.

AU

EF

Like the cartwheels and indeed a high proportion of the obverses listed here, the berries and the laurel leaves are crucial to grading these coins. In EF condition, just the merest flattening of the berries and rubbing of the outer leaf edges is permissible.

VF

Some wear on the curls over the ears typifies this grade, and the higher portions of the material around the shoulders also betray some erosion. The leaves will however retain some detail.

F

No detail left on the hair or leaves, and precious little on the toga. The hairline however should still be quite clear.

Fair

The outline of the head should still be visible whilst a little evidence of the laurel wreath is quite likely, and of course, the legend should still be legible.

Farthing, Halfpenny, Penny 1806-7

Due to the rising price of copper, the coins of 1806-7 were somewhat reduced in size, which together with their simpler form made them much more modern in appearance. These were the last base metal coins in which the two sides were set at 180 degrees to each other. Surprisingly coins with their general dimensions continued to be minted until 1860.

Superb proof penny in **FDC** condition

Slight wear above ear, on wreath and on clasp. **GEF** condition

EF

Early places to wear are the hair above the ear, the material running just off the horizontal from the clasp and the laurel leaves.

VF

Hair and ear merging. Clasp itself is now showing some wear.

F

Hair and wreath now blending together. Hair lines on crown much fainter and few folds remain in the material.

Fair

Due to it being heavily recessed, the eye is still clear, but there is little other detail on the head.

Actually the first modern silver coins, these used captured Spanish 8 Reales as blanks, and a careful look at a good specimen can often reveal the legend/design of the previous coin – a date is actually said to make the coin more valuable.

Wear most evident on laurel berries. **EF** condition

EF

A nice 'busy' design with plenty of high points to reveal its grade. Look first at the hair above the ear, the laurel wreath (including the berries) and the fabric around the king's neck.

VF

Many of the lower leaves will have flattened out although some will retain a degree of detail. Most of the folds in the cloth should still be visible.

F

The garment now lacks much detail, but most of the leaves and berries should still be clear.

Eighteen pence
Three shillings

These were semi-official coins issued by the bank to fill the gap left by the shortage of regular silver currency.

GEF. Very slight general wear. Check rivets at top of breastplate and stones on clasp

EF

Many points of detail, so not that difficult to spot the signs of early wear. Look especially above the eye and at the curls covering the ear.

VF

The curls above the ear and the laurel leaves are showing significant signs of wear. Erosion on the nose and eyebrow is also obvious.

F

All the high points have eroded to the point where the underlying design is unclear.

Eighteen pence
Three shillings

A much more modern portrait than that originally used, these were minted between 1812 and 1816 (scarce). They did not circulate for long, being withdrawn from circulation by 1820 and are therefore seldom found in badly worn condition.

AU

EF

Detail on leaves and berries should be quite bold. Possible slight wear on ear lobes and hair, especially below wreath.

VF

Leaves are showing far less detail and berries are hard to discern.

F

No detail on wreath which is merging with ear. Few hairlines on top of head, and only the deeper lines show below wreath.

Half Crown

Benedetto Pistrucci's portraits for the Royal Mint are characterised by the bold and frequently unflattering treatment of his ageing subjects, always executed in classical form with the traditional laurel wreath. This was an era of frequent changes in the coinage, there being no less than nine different portraits in the years 1816-30.

The so-called 'Bull Head' was hardly popular at the time, hence its early replacement, but, removed from public sympathy for an ailing monarch, can now be seen as a fine piece of work in its own right.

As a result of the robust style of engraving typical of its designer, the Bull Head shows great resistance to wear.

Head of **EF** coin close up. Wear most obvious on leaves, berries and in hair

EF

The leaves that form the laurel wreath are engraved in some detail with not only the central stalk, but clearly defined veins to either side. In EF grade, these should for the most part be bold and clear with perhaps the beginnings of wear showing on the higher points.

VF

The leaves are still bold, but the individual veins are now disappearing. The hair too is beginning to erode with many of the finer lines disappearing especially at the crown.

F

The individual leaves are still discernable but little detail remains, although the ear and the curl in front of it are still quite bold.

Fair

Little detail remaining although the robust rim keeps the legend from being worn away.

Sovereign, Half Sovereign, Half Crown

A rather kinder image of George III, this portrait replaced the unpopular 'Bull Head' design used on the half crown during 1816 and the earlier months of 1817. Gold coins of the new type were not issued until 1817 and all George III sovereigns and half sovereigns carried this obverse.

EF. Slight wear in leaves

EF

Unlike the Bull Head, the detail on the laurel leaves is limited to a central stalk which will still be present on all the leaves of a coin in this grade, even if slight wear is beginning to show on their outer edges.

VF

The central leaves lack detail, and the hair is beginning to erode on the crown. The ear too is beginning to pick up some wear.

F

The laurel leaves are still largely discernable and some of the broader hairlines remain visible, especially below the wreath.

Fair

Generally speaking, the legend should still be complete in this grade, although with the exception of the ear, the portrait lacks almost any detail.

Shilling/Sixpence

Not quite a reduced 'Bull Head', the design used on the lesser silver coinage in this period was perhaps the most robust of all British obverse portraits.

AU

EF

Like all the designs by Pistrucci, the first wear often shows itself in the laurel leaves, which should all clearly show the central stalk. You should also check the curl to the right of the ear.

VF

The central stalk will still be apparent on a majority of leaves (the leaf just above the ear can wear first).

F

Laurel leaves still bold for the most part, but one or two may be beginning to merge with the hair. Wear is becoming more general.

Fair

Little detail, but the ear still remains visible. The reverse of this coin is truly horrible.

Crown

Used not only on the crown, but also on the proof £2 and £5 pieces, this is the most flattering of Pistrucci's portraits of the, by then, old and insane monarch. Clearly a sitting was out of the question, and therefore the engraver seems to have produced an idealised portrait of the king as he was forty or more years before. According to Michael A Marsh,* these coins were treated with great care by the mint even down to being struck by a series of graduated blows, rather than the single blow which would normally be used for currency pieces; they were eventually issued to banks wrapped in soft paper.

All leaf veins visible indicating **AU** condition

Michael A Marsh – Benedetto Pistrucci Principal Engraver & Chief Medalist of the Royal Mint; 1783-1855

EF

As is usual with any laureate bust, the outer edges of the leaves are among the first points to wear, but there is plenty here to use in an assessment of the coin.

VF

Not all the leaves will now have their centre vein visible, and some of the higher hairlines will have disappeared. The unusually bold beading will also be beginning to wear.

F

The laurel wreath and some of the hairlines should still be visible, although there will now be considerable wear above and behind the eye.

Fair

Wreath now unclear, but there may still be some hairlines. All but the vestige of the eye will probably have disappeared.

Sovereign, Half Sovereign, Crown, Half Crown, Shilling, Sixpence

A bold, durable image by Pistrucci, which famously was disliked by the monarch. In retrospect, it is a triumph of realism, but one which ultimately cost the Italian engraver his job.

UNC. A good strike and practically as it left the mint

EF

Look out for the integrity of the veins in the laurel leaves. The hair at the temple can also wear quite early on as can the cheekbone.

VF

The more exposed leaves will now be missing their veins and many of the hair lines below the wreath will have disappeared.

F

All the leaves will still be clearly defined, but the hairline below the wreath may be less so. Increasingly noticeable wear on the cheek.

Fair

Few leaves whole and separate, and hairline has in all probability, completely disappeared. Can still be surprisingly clear in this grade, but the reverse may well be suffering more.

Farthing

Very similar to the image on the silver/gold coinage, but with the vestiges of a toga visible at the bottom of the design. The laurel wreath appears not to be so bold, but still holds much detail well into the lower grades.

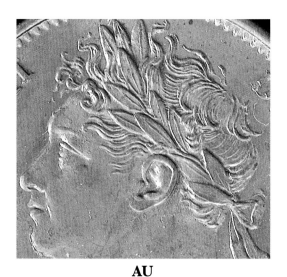

AU

EF. Slight wear on laurel leaves

EF

Largely as per the design used for the silver coinage, wear may first be seen on the laurel wreath, but the clasp can also wear early in its life.

VF

Few leaf veins visible, but wreath still intact in this grade.

F

Vestiges of wreath and clasp still visible in fine, whilst the ear is quite prominent.

Fair

Some detail persists in the lowest grade, although the state of preservation hardly makes it an attractive proposition.

Sovereign, Half Sovereign, Crown, Half crown, Shilling, Sixpence

Following Benedetto Pistrucci's dispute with the Royal Mint, William Wyon was instructed to produce a new obverse design based on a bust by Francis Chantrey. Despite its unfortunate origins, the result was a thoroughly satisfactory likeness of the ageing king which persisted until his death in 1830.

Slight cabinet friction just drops this coin down to **GEF**

EF

Assessing this design in the higher grades is a question of checking for slight rubbing of the hair (which, not being protected by a laurel wreath, wears quite rapidly). The most usual place for this to start is at the point just above the ear, which should itself also be checked, especially at the top.

VF

The hair is now showing distinct signs of wear, despite most of the larger hairlines still being intact.

F

Some hairlines will still be visible and the eye should be quite clear. The 'G' of 'Georgius' which seems to have dissapeared in this photograph is in fact still present on the original coin.

Fair

Mostly flat, but the ear can persist even beyond fair.

Third farthing, Half farthing, Farthing, Halfpenny, Penny

Very similar to Wyon's bare-head design used on the later George IV silver. Much more hard-wearing however, due to the protective effect of the laurel wreath.

Detail of a proof coin with just the slightest wear to its highest points, **GEF** condition.

Very close to **AU**, but slight cabinet friction means **GEF.**

EF

Check leaves of laurel wreath for signs of early wear. The ribbon on the neck can also wear prematurely.

VF

Laurel wreath still visible in its entirety. Ribbon may be worn where it crosses neck.

F

Obvious wear on wreath. Only deeper hairlines remain.

Fair

Wear continues as before. Likely to be considerably less worn than reverse.

Sovereign, Half Sovereign, Half Crown, Shilling, Sixpence, Fourpence, Threepence, Three Halfpence, Penny, Halfpenny, Farthing, Half Farthing, Third Farthing

'I've never slept with a queen before' were reputedly the first words of William, the former Duke of Clarence & St. Andrew's as king. 'Silly Billy' or latterly 'The Sailor King' turned out to be a far better monarch than many had feared, handling the constitutional crisis which arose out of the Great Reform Bill with no little skill, despite his failing health.

Although he died without legitimate heir, several descendants emanating from his relationship with the actress Dorothea Bland have attained fame in their own right. These include politician David Cameron, broadcaster Adam Hart-Davis and the late actor Oliver Reed.

The coinage issued during his reign was mainly notable for its uniformity, no major design alterations being made at all during the seven years he occupied the throne, in marked contrast to the seemingly constant changes which occurred during his brother's tenure. The obverse portrait by William Wyon followed the pattern set for George IV and although a fine piece of work, could be said to have flattered the ageing king.

EF

Look for the first signs of wear in the higher parts of the hair and above the eye.

VF

Wear is now becoming obvious, especially in the hair, and although flattened, most of the lines should still be evident. The ear too can begin to show signs of flattening.

F

Some hairlines still visible, although many of the more minor ones have now disappeared. Wear continues above the eye, which changes the expression on the king's face, giving him a slightly worried look and if anything ages the portrait.

Fair

Nearly all detail has now gone, although the ear remains long after all other distinguishing features have disappeared.

Quarter Farthing, Third Farthing, Half Farthing, Farthing, Halfpenny, Penny, Three Halfpence, Twopence, Threepence, Fourpence, Sixpence, Shilling, Half Crown, Crown, Half Sovereign, Sovereign

William Wyon's portrait of the young Queen Victoria is one of the most enduring images of the entire British series, and was ultimately produced for an unprecedented 49 years. Like the bun design, engraved by Wyon's son Leonard, the image was subtly changed over the years to at least partially reflect the queen's advancing age, although by the time of its replacement, it could hardly be said to represent a true likeness. The crowns, produced from 1839-47 had a pattern engraved on the hair bands while most other denominations were left plain.

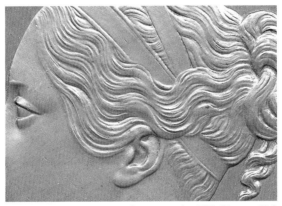

Detail from 1839 proof penny in **FDC** condition

EF. Slight wear beginning to show especially in the hair where it covers the hairbands

EF

This is not the easiest design to judge, the difference between the higher grades relying to a large extent on erosion in the hair. Copper coins at least give some clues with their toning but silver and gold can be more difficult. You may have more luck with the reverse.

VF

Wear in the higher points of the hair where it is loosely tied up at the back of the head (it is <u>not</u> a bun) has become much more obvious. The hair bands should still be distinctly visible on the top of the head.

F

A few hairlines left and only the vestiges of the hair bands remain.

Fair

What was once a portrait of a beautiful young woman has now become a singularly unattractive outline, with a few hairlines and the remains of the ear still visible in most cases. Where possible, better to save your money and buy your Young Head coin in higher grade.

Crown, Florin

Another of William Wyon's masterpieces, this design first appeared on the famous Gothic crowns of 1847, on proof florins in 1848 and florins for circulation the following year. The so-called 'Godless' florins produced in these two years differ mainly in having latin rather than gothic script and a more conventional beading. Full of detail and not that hard to grade, both sides of the coins produced to this design wear rapidly.

AU

EF

The first place to look for wear is the plait of hair which loops round the queen's ear. In addition, the crown should also be checked as should the detail on the bodice, especially at the shoulder.

VF

Wear extends from the side of the head outwards, beginning to erode the ear. At this point the hairline should still be visible.

F

The front edge of the crown has merged with the head and the hairline is no longer visible. Still some detail on the crown and bodice.

Fair

Head now mostly flat although a little detail may still persist on the dress. The gothic legend is still visible in bold relief.

Penny, Halfpenny, Farthing

Although there are many slight variations in this obverse design, they do nonetheless fall into three distinct groups. The earliest which was current until 1874 is a particularly attractive design, and once the initial bugs had been eliminated, was generally well-struck with a wealth of detail. It is thus a comparatively easy coin to assess for wear. The second batch followed the general pattern of the first, but had been altered to make the queen appear older. However, as she was by then aged 56, it could be argued that the design was still some way behind the times. These coins are if anything, even more robustly engraved than the earlier type, with a particularly heavy treatment of the laurel wreath. This feature comes to dominate the entire appearance of the coin as the wearing process takes place.

The final manifestation of the bun penny appeared in 1881 and like the earliest coins of Elizabeth II had been struck in very low relief, resulting in the appearance of rapid wear and a headlong tumble through the grades. Curiously, halfpennies and farthings continued to be struck with a much more durable image.

As a footnote, the obverse used in the third-farthings produced for Malta between 1866 and 1885 was in essence a cut down version of the bun head.

AU. Close up of a bun penny in stunning condition, with almost no bag damage

EF penny showing slight wear in upper leaves, hair above eye and in bun

EF

Very slight wear to the laurel wreath, the hair above the eye and the highest points of the bun. The pattern on the dress should still be crisp and, in the larger coins, the word 'Honi' clearly readable on the shoulder.

VF

The laurel wreath and the hair generally has flattened somewhat, with the hairline possibly a little hazy. It should still be possible to discern the pattern on the dress, although considerable wear will still be evident in this area.

F

Considerable general wear. Some thicker hairlines above the eye should be visible, as should the edge of the laurel wreath, especially on pennies minted between 1874 and 1881. A small vestige of the dress pattern remains.

Fair

Perhaps a few hair lines still visible but the face is largely flat. Even the worst specimens of the earliest design will clearly show the fabric rose at the bust.

Sovereign, Half Sovereign, Crown, Double Florin, Half Crown, Florin, Shilling, Sixpence, Fourpence, Threepence

This design was not popular at the time of its introduction and has some distinct aesthetic shortcomings, but the amount of detail present makes it an excellent coin on which to learn your grading technique.

Detail from Jubilee halfcrown, practically as struck

EF

There are many high spots to be checked for wear, but the pearls and the lace around the queen's head should be particularly investigated. Curiously the medal on the queen's shoulder appears to be cut in much sharper relief on the halfcrown and then persists in quite distinct form some way down the grading scale.

VF

Both the lace and the hairline should still be intact.

F
Much detail now missing, but the ear and earring will remain in evidence, as will much of the beading.

Fair
Face flat with ear and earring merging into face. A few heavy folds still visible on the veil.

Sovereign, Half Sovereign, Crown, Half crown, Florin, Shilling, Sixpence, Threepence, Penny, Halfpenny, Farthing

This was the final obverse design for the British coinage during Victoria's reign, and was a generally well-received and successful design. Grading is once again fairly straightforward with plenty of detail to assess.

Old head penny in **AU** condition
with a high percentage of lustre

EF

The first parts to show wear are likely to be the stones on the crown, the necklace and the garter star but almost any high point can receive some rubbing.

VF

Some hairlines remain and the garter star is still clearly visible on the queen's dress.

F

Just the faintest outline of the garter star, but all coins in fine and above will have an indication of the hairline.

Fair

Face essentially flat but some details may remain.

Sovereign, Half Sovereign, Crown, Half Crown, Florin, Shilling, Sixpence, Threepence, Penny, Halfpenny, Farthing, Third Farthing

Now this is where it starts getting difficult. It is one thing to assess a female image with plenty of ornamentation, quite another to judge the wear on the unadorned effigy of a balding man in his sixties. This is not to say that G W de Saulles' image was badly executed in any way – indeed it was a very good likeness, but to be blunt, the raw material was somewhat lacking.

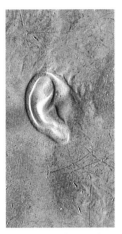

AU with slight bag abrasions

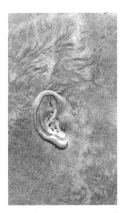

EF halfpenny showing beginnings of wear on upper ear

EF

A nice bronze image here shows the areas of early wear i.e. the hair just in front and above the ear, parts of the beard and the upper ear itself.

VF

The edge of the bald patch should still be distinct (the photograph does not unfortunately, do this feature justice). There are still plenty of hairlines in the upper parts of the beard and the ear is relatively untouched.

F

Still a few hairlines visible towards the back of the head and under the chin; once again the ear is still distinct.

Fair

No obvious hairlines visible and erosion is beginning to affect the ear and the eye.

Sovereign, Half Sovereign, Half Crown, Florin, Shilling, Sixpence, Threepence, Penny, Halfpenny, Farthing, Third Farthing

It should be noted that the low relief of these coins makes them some of the hardest obverses to grade accurately. During and immediately after the First World War, the average standard of strike, particularly of the bronze coins reached a low ebb with the reverse showing severe ghosting and both sides suffering from a lack of detail. It is probable that this reduction in standards came about due to the effects of the war (shortage of steel for dies, key staff on active service etc.) and as such was quite understandable. It is noticeable that coins issued prior to 1915 and after 1920 are generally of a much higher quality, although the ghosting is still known to occur outside these dates.

AU

EF. Slight wear on upper ear

EF

Wear is quite general, but the upper ear is diagnostic. Ends of the moustache and eyebrow can also suffer.

VF

Obvious erosion along the side of the face as well as the points mentioned above. Hairline should still be visible back to the temple. Hairlines in moustache have now largely disappeared.

F

Whole side of face worn flat, hair lines now missing from moustache. Hairline no longer visible at temple.

Fair

Very little detail other than lower ear, eye and beard.

Sovereign, Crown, Half Crown, Florin, Shilling, Sixpence, Threepence, Penny, Halfpenny, Farthing

Essentially a re-cut version of the original Bertram Mackennal engraving, the standards of production by this stage had improved dramatically, and this is actually one of the most consistent obverse images in the British series. There is a little more detail, but grading can still cause problems for the uninitiated.

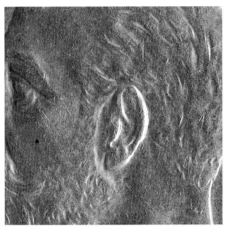

GEF

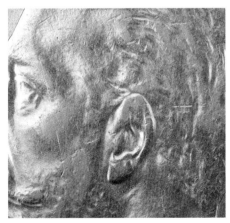

EF

EF

Same grading points as for the original head, but there are more hairlines which gradually disappear as the coin descends the grades.

VF

Still many hairlines visible and as before, the hairline at the temple should be clear. If anything, the ear wears even more quickly than on the earlier series.

F

The truncation can become indistinct, top of ear has merged with head. Some hairlines still visible in beard.

Fair

Very little detail discernable other than the ear and the obvious moustache.

Crown, Half Crown, Florin, Shilling, Sixpence, Threepence (Silver), Threepence (Brass), Penny, Halfpenny, Farthing

A completely unadorned portrait of the current queen's father by T. Humphrey Paget who had also designed the effigy for his brother's coinage. Arguably easier to grade than any of the circulation portraits produced since the days of Queen Victoria.

The 'silver' coins minted from 1947 to 1952 are in cupro-nickel and wear less readily than the earlier coins with a 50% silver content. They and the bronze denominations are seldom seen as low as 'fair'.

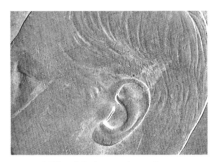

AU with bag abrasions

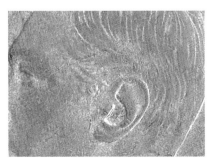

EF. Discolouration showing location of early wear

EF

All of the fine hairlines running from top to bottom of the portrait should be visible. The first place for the coin to wear tends to be the eyebrow.

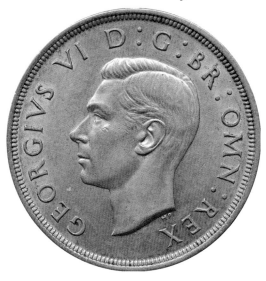

VF

Many of the less pronounced hairlines will have disappeared, although those above the parting should still be visible, as well as coarse lines running from left to right above the ear.

F

Signs of substantial wear on side of face, although the coarse hairlines above remain just visible.

Fair

Little detail still visible, even the ear is becoming less defined. Few coins wore more than that depicted here.

Sovereign, Crown, Half Crown, Florin, Shilling, Sixpence, Threepence, Penny, Halfpenny, Farthing

After a run of four kings on the trot, the engravers of Britain were, for the first time in ninety years, faced with the prospect of producing a likeness of a young woman.

The design chosen was by Mary Gillick, an elderly artist of the New-lyn school. It is a portrait of the queen wearing a simple and barely discernable dress, and surprisingly a laurel wreath – a revival of a tradition which last saw light of day on the 'bun' coinage of 1860.

The cut of the dies produced in the first year of her reign was far too shallow and after thirty years of circulation, many of the coins produced from them ended up almost featureless. From 1954 however, the design was re-cut and the result became far more durable.

AU

EF. Wear most obvious in leaves on upper part of laurel wreath

EF

The key to wear on this design lies in the berries on the laurel wreath which begin to flatten after a very short period of circulation. The leaves themselves also wear on their outer edges. In view of the frequently poor quality of the finished product, it can be extremely difficult and at times practically impossible, to distinguish between EF and AU.

VF

Leaves and berries considerably flattened.

F

Just the vestiges of the wreath and very little other detail remaining. Shillings and florins circulated for longer than their contemporaries, and are more likely to be encountered in this condition.

THE REVERSES

Arrangement of Reverses:

Twopence, Penny

This was the first Britannia of the modern era, and perhaps surprisingly, it closely followed that of 1672, when the Duchess of Richmond modelled for the first official milled copper coinage. The introduction of the man-of-war in the background set the pattern for future developments in which any pretence of Britannia as the peace-maker was dropped, losing her olive branch and donning a Greco-Roman helmet along the way.

As with the obverse, the rim takes a lot of damage and to some extent protects the design from wear.

GEF. Wear most noticeable on side of face and breast

EF

The protective effect of the rim tends to make wear on the actual design somewhat general, but check the head, the left breast, the left leg and of course the rim for signs of early wear.

VF

This and the next picture show how general wear can be. Twopences (as here) tend to show wear on the shield, whereas pennies are more likely to exhibit erosion on the head and upper body.

F

Ensure that the integrity of the figure is maintained and that the word 'Britannia' and the date can still be read in their entirety.

Fair

Legend still legible but unsurprisingly, beginning to wear. Design heavily eroded. Some erosion of legend is acceptable in this unusual design.

Farthing, Halfpenny

The design on the reverse of these coins is very similar to that on the cartwheel pennies/twopences but with a more conventional rim and beading. Grading hints tend to follow those for the Cartwheel series. Although the rim is nowhere near as bulky as on the earlier coin, it is nonetheless fairly robust and remains largely intact well beyond fine.

1806 proof halfpenny in **FDC** condition

GEF. Slight wear on fingers and on left breast

EF

Erosion can be fairly general but early wear points are likely to include the side of the head, the left breast and the ground line.

VF

F

Fair

Like the cartwheel series this was designed by C H Küchler. Britannia is set in a tableau rather like the reverse of the bronze bun series, but far from being surrounded by symbols of the sea, we must assume that she is now seated in a field, accompanied by a cornucopia and a beehive. This is not an unattractive image but it only takes up the centre portion of the coin, the outside being reserved for the legend and value in two concentric rings.

An oddity of these coins is that the edge is left plain.

UNC

EF. Wear evident on side of face, breasts and arms

EF

Minute wear on the face and left breast. As normal, the fingers will also reveal some slight rubbing.

VF

Face flattened, edge of shield becoming less distinct. The legend 'Five Shilling Dollar' is already beginning to show signs of wear. Shaft of spear just distinct over shoulder.

F

Horizontal lines behind inner legend have worn away in places; shaft of spear has eroded into shoulder.

Fair

This is one of those coins that wears from the inside out i.e. Britannia and the inner legend (Five Shillings Dollar) heading for oblivion long before the outer legend and the beading.

Farthing

This design only appeared on farthings minted between 1821 and 1826. Actually a rather pleasant design, it does suffer from having too much detail in too small a space. Not only does Britannia have to cope with an olive branch and a shield in her right hand whilst holding a trident in her left, but the engraver has also positioned her beside a lion, whose head is visible in the bottom right hand corner.

AU

EF. Slight wear on helmet and right breast

EF

Some slight wear on helmet, right breast and on the drapery covering the shield.

VF

Shield design largely intact and individual waves just above the exergue are still visible.

F

Just a small portion of the shield design is visible.

Fair

Trident shaft and hand are tending to disappear. Almost no design left on shield.

Fourpence, Penny, Halfpenny, Farthing, Half Farthing, Third-Farthing

This was a long lived design which was produced during three reigns, appeared on no less than six different denominations and was in fact the only reverse design in our period to appear on both base metal and silver coinage. Unlike its successor, Britannia sits alone without background or accoutrements other than her shield and trident. When in tip-top condition, this is one of the highlights of the entire British series. Unfortunately however, it does not wear attractively with too much erosion occurring on the upper body, producing a curious rag doll-like effect.

FDC. Reverse of 1839 proof penny

EF. Obvious wear in hair, on right breast and on fingers

Detail from exergue of halfpenny in **AU** condition

EF

Helmet and fingers show early wear as does the rose in the exergue, but the area which undoubtedly erodes first is the right breast.

VF

Incuse lines on thistle no longer visible.

F

Despite the shield being convex in section, the whole of the union jack should still be visible to the naked eye.

Fair

Legend on right (usually) becoming indistinct as is tip of trident. Higher parts of shield showing wear.

Penny, Halfpenny, Farthing

In this design, Britannia rules the waves against a backdrop of a sailing ship, a lighthouse and some rocks. This was another attractive and long-lived design seeing service on the three major bronze denominations. Designed by L C Wyon and always in partnership with his 'bun' head, the languid pose is somewhat at odds with our perception of the rather severe culture which existed in the latter part of the nineteenth century.

In common with its obverse partner, there are many variations on the basic theme. This is particularly noticeable on the penny, and from a grading point of view the most significant is in the shape of the shield. In 1860 and 1861 most coins were produced with a flat shield. From the latter part of 1861 coins began to be produced with a distinctly convex profile which persisted until 1882 when the mint reverted to a flat design. The convex shield wears readily and is a handy tool in assessing the grade, whereas a coin with a flat shield has to be in pretty dreadful condition to betray any wear in this area at all! All the following photographs use convex shield pennies.

AU

EF. Slight wear in hair, plumes, folds of dress and on fingers

EF

Slight wear on the fingers, the hair below the helmet and, where present, the convex shield. The design is very detailed and individual coins can show slight wear in many different areas. Due to their size, one should not expect anywhere near as much detail on the halfpenny or particularly, the farthing.

VF

Individual toes may just be visible, but the left forearm is taking on a very flat appearance.

F

The foot is now flat but individual bricks may still be discerned on the lower part of the lighthouse.

Fair

The ship has now become a mere outline and much of the design is now flat.

Penny, Halfpenny, Farthing

The world moves on and banishes the square rigger to history. It is not clear though, why the lighthouse too goes the way of the lion and the olive branch and Britannia now rules a meagre bit of sea with only the rocks for company. This was the last version of Britannia to appear on the halfpenny and farthing, and was moreover the last reverse design to appear concurrently on more than one denomination. Another essentially well-executed image, it did at times suffer drastically from poor standards of production, the head and right shoulder being particularly susceptible. The severe 'ghosting' from the obverse took many years to correct.

The final versions of this design, produced from 1927-36 are particularly pleasing, with all incuse lines well cut and the whole presentation being made to a much higher standard of workmanship. Moreover, they wear especially well, seldom being seen in less than 'fine' condition.

AU

EF. Light but obvious wear on fingers, face, upper arm and right breast

EF

Fingers and helmet are diagnostic in indicating the first signs of wear. The right breast too can show signs of erosion, but beware as this area is often not fully struck up.

VF

Wear extends to the right shoulder and the first signs are now present on the shield, but the union jack should still be complete on any coin in this grade.

F

Any semblance of individual fingers will now have disappeared and the union jack is in all probability no longer clear.

Fair

Just a little detail remaining on the lowest parts of the face, the body and under the leg, everywhere else being largely flat.

Penny

This is the last incarnation of Britannia in our period. Although a generally satisfactory design, it appears to lack the lightness of touch apparent in its predecessors, and quite why the trident has now shrunk into a toasting fork is anybody's guess! On the plus side, the lighthouse once again graces the left side of the coin, but the pose adopted by Britannia seems excessively stiff and uncomfortable in marked contrast to the relaxed positions of her predecessors. With separate designs for the halfpenny and farthing, Britannia is now confined to the penny.

The sea in the later dies of Elizabeth II was progressively re-cut to give a 'rough sea' effect. This was perhaps a little heavy-handed and did not sit well with the comparative realism of the foreground.

AU

EF. Slight wear on right breast

EF

Slight wear on fingers, helmet and right breast. Detail on this design is not always fully struck up and moreover, it can be plagued with bag abrasions.

VF

Obvious wear in the aforementioned places, which now extends down the right leg and to the waves just above the exergue.

F

Wear in pretty much the same places although more severe. Few coins descended beyond this point.

Edward VII ascended the throne on 22 January 1901 and although other denominations remained the same or reverted to well-used themes, the florin was singled out for a radical overhaul and what emerged was startlingly new and different. Britannia (rarely seen on silver coins) was depicted in art nouveau style standing in the prow of a stylised ship against the backdrop of a heavy sea; her robes billowing out behind her in the breeze.

Many people would regard this as their favourite British coin design, but it was only produced for the nine short years of Edward VII's reign. Certainly had it continued, it would have been out of step with the more sombre era that followed.

Sadly, resistance to wear is woeful.

GEF. Tiny amount of wear/damage to breast

EF

Wear tends to be rather general, but in the first instance, check the helmet and the prow of the ship.

VF

In addition to the above, the folds of the dress wear at the point where they cover the left thigh. As Britannia's face is presented in three-quarters view, the nose becomes the highest point and wears before the rest of the face.

F

The ship is now essentially flat and extensive wear can be seen on the fabric of the dress. The right side of the face is likely to be featureless.

Fair

Britannia is now little more than an outline but, somewhat unusually the date on this coin is still identifiable. Many examples, even those that would otherwise be described as 'fine' tend to suffer from localised erosion, completely obliterating the last figure of the date, at which point they are effectively scrap.

Sovereign, Crown

Although the George & Dragon design lasted a mere four years in its original form, it represented a return to a more imaginative era in coin design, and bore more than a passing resemblance to the angel designs current from the late middle ages until the defeat of Charles I.

It is a moot point whether the design was improved by the subsequent deletion of the garter and heavy beading, but nonetheless it represents one of greatest designs ever to appear on a British coin.

The design appears **AU**, but the scratches in the field may indicate some cleaning in the past.

EF

There is a little difference in the wear encountered on the two versions of George and the dragon; the most obvious being that the strap across the body does not wear as readily on the earlier version.

VF

Wear becomes obvious on the heads of both St. George and his horse. Wear on the body is more apparent on the dragon.

F

Fair

Sovereign, Half Sovereign, Crown

It would not be stretching the truth to describe this design as an all-time classic. Although the original design was a marvellous piece of engraving in its own right, Benedetto Pistrucci's George & Dragon did not attain its familiar and enduring form until 1820 when the garter was deleted (on the pattern £2 and £5 pieces) to reveal the engraver's art in almost medal-like form.

It is true that the dragon appears to be about the size of a labrador and more likely to be a minor nuisance than the terror of legend, and why England's patron saint deemed it appropriate to don a helmet, a cape, a pair of boots and pretty much nothing else to tackle the beast can only be the subject of conjecture. Be that as it may, this is a stunning piece of work which has transcended mere coinage to become nothing less than a potent symbol of nationhood.

GEF. Showing very slight wear on the side of the helmet and strap where it crosses the chest

A little more wear on this **EF** example

EF

Look for slight wear on the helmet above the eye and side of torso where the body is crossed by a leather strap. Fingers on both hands should be clear.

VF

Rein over horse's neck still intact if slightly worn; sword stands proud of flank

F

Wear begins to merge the point of the sword with the horse's flank and there will be very little detail left on the horse's face, although that of both the dragon and St. George will still retain some distinct features.

Fair

George and the dragon are now nothing more than a mere outline, although the beading should still be intact even in this grade.

Another bold move by the mint, for not only was this an ultra-modern design, but it was unashamedly issued simply as a one-off to commemorate a single event. Opinions on the design have been mixed, but you could not fault the mint's bravery in producing it.

Not technically a circulating coin, so it barely qualifies for inclusion, but quite a number seem to have found their way into the pockets of the population where they stayed jingling around with the loose change until they started to descend the grading tables. Not uncommon in VF but rarely much worse than that.

This coin is technically **AU** despite being plagued with abrasions

EF

Few sharp points to the design, so little to give away early wear. The highest point is the shield which does show wear, but as it is curved and in very low relief, could take some time with a magnifying glass to establish the level of erosion.

VF

Cross on shield will be only partially discernable, as will side of St. George's head. Reins should still be visible in their entirety. Lines indicating hairs will still just be visible in tail.

Shilling, Sixpence

In an odd way I actually rather like this one. It was engraved at a time when an artist couldn't just pop down to Longleat to see a real live lion and the final result looks like a small dog with short front legs, hugely oversized paws, and a distinctly human face. On the other hand it is a welcome change from all those shields and the design certainly has character. Perhaps I just don't get heraldry, but surely the concept of a wild animal wearing a crown is in itself fundamentally risible. In most cases the creature's indignity is well hidden as it remains firmly in the background but here, centre stage, the poor thing looks distinctly uncomfortable.

AU

EF

There are plenty of clues to the grading process here; the lion's face, the rose and thistle, the jewels in the crown... Actually a very easy coin to judge; lower grades just continue the theme.

VF

F

Fair

Shilling 1902-26
Sixpence 1911-26

After an absence of 73 years, the solitary lion returns in leaner and meaner form. Manifestly from the same stable as the standing Britannia, the lion is much more recognisably of its species than its late-Georgian predecessor, even if one does miss the wealth of detail in the earlier design. All in all however, a thoroughly competent and well-executed piece of engraving.

AU

EF. Slight wear on lion's nose and stones at base of crown

EF

Early wear will be evident on the lion's nose, front paws, orb and stones on the crown.

VF

The tail will have lost much detail although some will remain in the mane. Facial features still quite clear.

F

Main features still plain, even if in this coin, the face displays substantial wear.

Fair

Edge encroaching on outer parts of lettering. Detail on crown becoming indistinct.

Shilling 1927-36
English Shilling 1937-51

An update on the by now, traditional lion and crown type reverse, but with a much more upright lion projecting through the legend at the top. The design survived in slightly amended form to become the 'English' shilling from 1937-51, the major difference being the repositioning of the date to the field on either side of the lion.

UNC

EF

The facial features of the lion, the orb and the stones on the crown are diagnostic.

VF

The face is now rather flat but most other parts of the design retain a good amount of detail.

F
Look for extensive erosion on the crown and the tail.

Fair
Some detail on the centre portion of the crown but almost none on the lion. In this example, the lettering is also becoming rubbed.

'Scottish' Shilling

The concept of the Scottish shilling is a strange one, because if all shillings issued in Scotland were of the Scottish type, and likewise all shillings issued in England were of the English type, then due to their relative populations, English shillings would have outnumbered Scottish by some twelve to one, which is palpably not the case. In fact the relative mintages were not far from parity. Nonetheless, it did add a little variety to the coinage during a very dark time.

The coin clearly bears a family resemblance to its English cousin, and likewise wear should be investigated in similar places; the lion's face, jewels on the crown and additionally in the Scottish version the thistle can provide some clues.

AU

EF. Slight but obvious wear on thistle

EF

In EF grade the thistle on the right hand side of the lion will show a very slight flattening at its highest points; the orb atop the crown may also show a little wear.

VF

In addition to the above, the fingers(!) will be showing some wear as in all probability, will the lower ends of the sword/staff.

F

It is easy to spot the differences in wear between the previous picture and this one – fingers, thistle, sword, crown; all show a marked deterioration from the coin in VF condition.

A rather uninspired design but wear on the roses and thistles makes it easier than most of its contemporaries to grade.

AU

EF

EF

The easiest point at which to see any wear is in the centre of the rose which will just appear slightly less sharp than a coin in AU condition.

VF

The stamen in the middle of the rose are for the most part individually visible. Wear is however increasing on the thistle and the edges of the shamrock have flattened substantially.

F

Considerable general wear. Note the centre of the rose is now more or less flat.

Fair

The crown in this design is virtually indestructable, but the rose, shamrock and thistle are all showing heavy wear as is the rim.

A somewhat intricate piece of work in which the legend fits into convenient gaps in the design. Again however, the thistles and rose make grading a comparatively straightforward process. Having a direct decimal equivalent, it was not necessary to withdraw the florin in 1971, this series finally being replaced in 1992 with the new small size 10p piece. The wear evident on many examples can therefore exceed that on the contemporary bronze coinage.

AU

EF

EF

Just the slightest wear will be evident on the stamen (centre) of the rose, very little evident elsewhere.

VF

The stamen will still be individually visible, but wear here is obvious, as it is on the higher points of the thistles.

F

The centre of the rose is now largely featureless as are higher points of the design elsewhere. The engraved parts of the coin now have a very flat appearance.

This was the design which introduced the garter surrounded by ribbons and yet more garters enclosing a rose, a theme which was to soldier on into the twentieth century. The tiny George & Dragon below the design also made its debut. Quite involved for its time, it does provide many clues to help the collector.

Close up of the **EF** specimen showing wear points at base of shield

EF

The George and dragon is a good place to start; this should still be clear and moreover the lance should be visible throughout its entire length as should the leg of St. George. The faces of the lions may have begun to wear slightly, although the eyes, which in this design are merely holes, should still be clear on most if not all.

VF

Wear becomes apparent on the small roses within the garters. St. George and the dragon are less clear.

F

The motto 'Honi Soit…' will have worn to the extent that it is only just readable, but every stone at the bottom of the crown should be individually visible.

Fair

Only random letters in the motto will still be visible, and wear on the rim may well have begun to encroach. The crown is likely to be a mere outline.

This coat of arms can hardly be described as shield shape, being almost as wide as it is high. The devices themselves are rather crudely formed which has an effect on the grading.

UNC. There is little detail in the lions' faces but this is due to the comparatively small size of the coin rather than wear or any die weakness.

EF

Check for wear on the crown and the harp's breast. Other high points too should be checked for minute wear.

VF

The rather ill-formed devices wear rapidly, especially the harp which will already have become little more than a silhouette. By contrast, the diminutive Hanoverian shield seems to be well protected.

F

Unlike some shield designs, the motto is quite readable in this grade, although there is much wear within the shield.

Fair

The devices are becoming rather fuzzy and the motto has been completely rubbed off in places.

Change for change's sake? Although the Bull Head was said to be unpopular with the great unwashed, it is likely that they never gave the reverse a second glance. Nonetheless, the reverse was re-designed, deleting the outer ring of garters and ribbons together with St. George and the Dragon, giving rather less for the coin collector to grade. This situation was made worse by the fact that the dies tended to block up in many of these early shield designs, leaving what at first glance looked like patches of isolated erosion.

EF. There is little detail in the lions' faces but this is due to the comparatively small size of the coin rather than wear or any die weakness

EF

The buckle and garter end at the very bottom of the coin can show early wear, and that good old standby, the lions' facial features should be inspected to ensure that the eyes, at least, are still intact.

VF

Much of the design is now flattening out, but check that most of the detail is still present on the small crown. The majority of the lions will still show the last vestiges of their eyeholes.

F

Once again the majority of the garter motto should still be legible, but much detail is missing elsewhere. As in its predecessor, the stones at the bottom of the crown should still be visible.

Fair

The legend is rather more prone to wear than is the case on the obverse, and total obliteration generally occurs from the rim inwards. As in other Hanoverian designs, the inescutcheon in the centre of the coin is among the last places to wear.

Half Crown, Shilling, Sixpence

This, in my view, is one of the more attractive of the many and varied shield reverses of the period. It wears well too, even outlasting the resilient laurel wreath type obverse which was mated with all these coins.

UNC

EF

There are many high points to check on this coin. In EF condition there may be a little wear on the thistle, the rose or the lions but almost anywhere can show some sign of rubbing.

VF

The thistle design is a little more robust than most, and consequently should show some detail in this grade. Within the shield however, much more wear will be evident with the lion, the harp and the Hanoverian crown all showing signs of significant erosion. The plumes surrounding the shield may also be showing signs of flattening.

F

The crown still shows its individual stones and the various items of vegetation retain enough detail to be more than mere outlines.

Fair

Wear is considerable but quite even. The word 'anno' and the date are extremely bold and even in this condition should not be showing much obvious erosion.

A very similar design to that which appeared on the reverse of the 'Bull Head' half-crowns. Wear patterns are very similar to those of the earlier coin.

EF

VF

F

Fair

A fairly ordinary shield, which like the contemporary half crown reverse was re-hashed in the late nineteenth century as part of Queen Victoria's Jubilee coinage. The sixpence in this latter set was hastily withdrawn when it was discovered that they were being gilded and passed off as half-sovereigns!

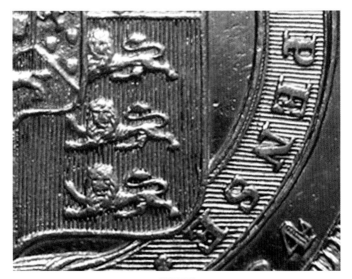

UNC

EF

The high points to check for early wear are lions' faces, orb (later coins) and stones on crown and buckle.

VF

The shield devices flatten quite readily in this design, but because of the bold beading, this wear is fairly evenly distributed throughout the coin. The step down from EF to VF can be very difficult to chart, but inspect the orb (where present), the fleurs de lys around the Scottish lion and moreover, the lettering of the motto, whilst at first glance being largely undamaged, will have flattened somewhat.

F

The harp is showing the most wear on both sets of coins. Once again, the Hanoverian inescutcheon on the earlier coins remains fairly bold.

Fair

Devices wearing away but even in this lowly condition, expect the motto to be perfectly readable.

No sooner had the public got used to one design than another came along to replace it. This however was a fine piece of engraving, the perspective on the delicate plumes flanking the shield being particularly masterful.

Proof halfcrown in **FDC** condition showing the mass of detail contained within this design

EF

The edges of the feathers are especially prone to early wear, as is the lower part of the helmet where it overlaps the shield. Also check the normal wear points such as the lion and the stones on the crown.

VF

Wear is quite general, but the uppermost of the lower set of lions will in all probability, now be somewhat unclear. The beginnings of wear around the word 'Mon' appears diagnostic.

F

In this grade, the motto, 'Dieu et mon droit' should still be perfectly legible, although the plumes will by now be flattening out.

Fair

Should still retain much detail, although the edge may be encroaching and the motto hard to discern.

This is a rather different treatment of the royal coat of arms. The garter is still there but is largely hidden below an ermine mantle which dominates the entire presentation, and gives a pleasing three-dimensional effect.

Possibly the most imaginative of the shield reverses, it does not however wear particularly well and in low grade, presents a large strangely shaped expanse of flat silver where the mantle had once been.

Shows considerable die weakness but otherwise **EF**

EF

A little wear in the usual places such as harp's breast and lions' faces. The mantle too will pick up some wear on its embroidered edge. This specimen is particularly poorly struck on the lower part of the harp, but this is a worn die – little to do with wear.

VF

The embroidery is worn away where it flanks the shield and the tassels at the end of the cords have lost all detail. However, most of the design points are still discernable on both the crown and the small George & Dragon motif at the bottom of the shield.

F

All detail has gone from the mantle except for the flecks at the bottom (ermine tails), where they are protected by the shield. Still a little detail on the crown but the inescutcheon in the centre has become badly worn.

Fair

The eroded mantle presents an almost ghostly aspect which dominates what detail remains. The crown shows little other than the outline, but still the ermine tails can be discerned under the shield.

Queen Victoria, by dint of being a woman, was unable to become Elector of Hanover and hence the inescutcheon disappeared from the royal coat of arms. This was a much simpler design than its predecessors with neither garter nor mantle but there is still plenty of detail to point you towards its grade.

EF

The three lions as always provide some clues, and somewhat unusually, so does the single Scottish lion rampant. The rose, thistle and shamrock too can help. On the five shilling piece especially, check the stones on the edge of the crown.

VF

Some leaves beginning to flatten and there is some wear towards the centre of the shield. The Scottish lion is quite flat.

F

Crowns in particular wear from the middle outwards, and it is not uncommon to see otherwise fine coins with the centre of the shield completely obliterated (downgrade immediately to fair). This however is a half crown which shows much more general wear. Look especially at the wreath and the harp.

Fair

Despite the obvious wear, the integrity of the design holds up well, at least in the half crown. See above for comments on the crown.

This was the one denomination where the reverse design did not markedly change on the introduction of the new Jubilee head. Gold currency was not allowed to deteriorate substantially whilst in circulation and therefore the vast majority of specimens fall into the VF-EF category. Coins in a true Fine are rare, and anything lower almost unheard of.

EF
Usual wear points; motifs within the shield, stones on the crown, beading etc.

VF

F

In essence this was a re-hash of the short-lived shield type which appeared on the George IV halfcrowns issued in 1823 and 1824; the most noticeable alterations being the removal of the arms of Hanover and the different shape of the crown. It was not the most inspired of designs, so it is difficult to understand why it was perpetuated in this way. Wear tends to be quite general with, as usual, the motto of the Order of the Garter (Honi Soit etc.) beginning to get a little faint by the time the coin hits fine.

UNC

EF

Those old standbys the lions' faces and the small George and Dragon (where the lance should be complete) can be used here. There is plenty of other detail to investigate.

VF

Obvious wear on the small garters and the large buckle. The faces of the lions may well be flat.

F

Some of the shield detail becoming blurred; the odd letter in the 'honi soit…' motto missing or only partially present.

Fair

Further blurring on the design itself. Wear on the rim is now likely to be encroaching on the legend.

Perhaps I have a penchant for Victoriana, but this strikes me as one of the most attractive of all the shield designs which have graced our coinage in the period 1816-1970, although if pressed I would struggle to say why. Certainly, there was nothing really new, even the ribbons and roses within individual garters that flank the shield were used as far back as 1816. Ultimately, I suppose it just comes down to the overall balance of the design and the competence of the engraving.

UNC

EF. Shows wear to George and Dragon and lower part of shield especially the lions passant

EF

As usual check out the lions in the shield and the jewels near the base of the crown. The small St. George and the Dragon at the base of the coin may have picked up a little more wear than would have been the case on the previous design.

VF

St. George & Dragon will be pretty worn. Inspect the pellets between the legend and the main design for slight flattening. The edges of the garters will be less clear than in the previous grade but a good test is to check that the buckles are still visible.

F

Coin very flat and as they stand slightly proud, the designs inside the shield are becoming somewhat misty.

Fair

Garters and crown are little more than an outline and although lions, harp etc. are just visible, there is no detail and indeed some parts may have been obliterated altogether.

Again one of the better shields, but like other denominations, it all goes horribly wrong in 1915 when the quality of many coins falls dramatically. There are actually two distinct reverses here, as the coins of George V lack the ring of pellets around the garter which denote the coins of Edward VII.

AU

EF

The edge of the shield and the line dividing its separate parts are among the first places to wear. The crown can also show early erosion at the bottom edge, but at this point, the lions show less wear than is evident in other designs.

VF

Wear is much more evident on the edge of the shield and the lions too are beginning to suffer. The letters of the motto have begun to look well rubbed, especially near the folds at 9 and 3 o'clock.

F
Getting much flatter, but the motifs are still largely separate from the shield edge.

Fair
This design has quite lightweight beading and wear will begin to infiltrate from the edge, resulting in the upper parts of the legend beginning to disappear.

Once again, there are slight differences between the coins produced for each of the two monarchs represented here but the designs are so closely related that there is little point in discussing them separately. The bold engraving means that they can be hard to judge, and frequently show a higher grade than the necessarily more organic designs on the obverse.

AU

EF

This is not a coin to check out the 'lion's face' grading technique, as they are very boldly struck and seldom wear like earlier coins. Check with a magnifying glass for minute damage to the body of the Scottish lion rampant. In the earlier coins, the thistle will provide some easy clues. All lines and the legend should be similarly checked for the beginnings of wear. In this particular coin, the uppermost lion does not appear to have been fully struck up.

VF

General wear, but check that the strip by which the shield hangs from the ring is still intact (George VI coins only).

F

A surprisingly large amount of detail will still exist. Look for the overlap of the interlocking Gs becoming merged, especially for some reason on the left. Few cupro-nickel coins (1947-on) will have descended beyond this.

Fair

As with most coins from this era and later, the design tends to wear flat, protected by its bold engraving and heavy beading. Everything will still be there but in heavily eroded form.

This would have been the reverse of Edward VIII's coronation crown had Wallis Simpson not intervened. Nice enough but essentially a conventional shield, the only break with tradition being the inclusion of the lion and the unicorn.

EF. Slight wear on chain where it crosses body

EF

The orb just underneath the cross gets some early wear, as does the chain where it crosses the unicorn's body. The lion outside the shield takes some rubbing, especially on the nose and the tongue.

VF

Most high points now flat. Chain, as above, will lack any detail.

The last half crown minted, and in terms of workmanship, sadly amongst the worst, with the area within the shield often appearing rough-hewn even when fresh from the mint. Moreover, this lack of detail continued throughout much of the production run. The design was traditional if a little bland, and all things considered was a poor swansong for a much loved coin.

AU

EF *There will be minute amounts of wear on high spots such as the orb on the crown immediately below the cross and the stones towards the bottom of the crown. This is not a coin which should be assessed purely on its reverse and, in better condition, more weight should be given to any wear on the obverse. Due to the frequently poor quality of the strike, it is inadvisable to use the three lions in the shield as a touchstone to grading this design.*

VF

Wear continuing in the above places, but also check out the scrolls flanking the lower part of the shield which will by now be beginning to show some wear on their higher points.

F

Much of the detail will have merged, and the design overall may have a rather flat appearance. You are unlikely to find many examples in much worse condition than that in this picture.

The concept of splitting shilling production into English and Scottish types was continued under Elizabeth II. The English coins used the familiar three lions within a simple crowned shield, surprisingly the first time this had been used in isolation on a circulating coin.

The design is in bold relief, and seldom turns up in less than VF condition. Grading however, is in most cases academic as anything below EF (with the possible exception of 1958) is to all intents and purposes, valueless.

AU

EF

Any wear is likely to show itself on the stones at the bottom of the crown, the nearby pellets and on the lions' faces. Expect evenings wasted with a magnifying glass to distinguish EF from AU.

VF

Almost anything else. Note that the pellet on the orb (under the upper cross) has been eroded away to nothing.

Very similar to its English counterpart, the one difference being the rampant Scottish lion within the shield. Grading notes can be taken as similar too, as the single lion is not particularly diagnostic where wear is concerned.

UNC

EF

VF

Gothic Crown 1847-53
Godless Florin 1848-87

The 'cruciform shields' design dated back to the days of Charles II, in subsequent years being enhanced by the addition of roses and/or plumes in the angles to denote the origin of the metal. Therefore, the design which first appeared on the 'Gothic' crown in 1847, and the florin (proof only) the following year was hardly new. What was novel however, was the intricate treatment of the subject, and other than the 'Godless' florins of 1848-9, the use of Gothic lettering in the legend.

The legendary crown performed little more than a toe in the water function, never being adopted for full scale circulation – but what stunning coins they were – even average examples now selling for well into four figures.

These are all attractive and popular coins but, partly due to three of the four shields having no discernable border, they do suffer from rapid wear.

GEF. Wear becoming obvious on lions passant. This is an area that can wear rapidly. However, apparent wear in this area can also be the result of die weakness

EF
The lions and the harp will already be showing slight wear as will the thistle and roses in the angles.

VF
Wear continues much as before with the outer lions wearing quite rapidly.

F

The lions' eyes will be disappearing, as will any detail on the crowns, but it is the contents of the shields which receive most rubbing.

Fair

To all intents and purposes the designs in the shields have now disappeared, but in most cases the wording will still be sharp and clear.

Although the Gothic crowns and florins had carried the torch for the concept of the cruciform shield, this was a return to a simpler interpretation, in essence one which had done sterling service for every monarch from Charles II to George III. In the past however, the sceptres had been restricted to the gold denominations. After the Gothic series, they appeared gaunt and unimaginative, and the double florin (or 'Barmaid's Ruin') was unpopular for other reasons. Detail on the Victorian florin is frequently lacking and the collector can search in vain for anything resembling a face on the English lions.

After the decline of the much maligned Jubilee head, the reverse of the florin went first to the almost baroque series which marked Queen Victoria's final years and then to the stunning 'Standing Britannia' of 1902-10. Although many mourned the decline of this brilliant image, the revival of the cruciform shield that followed aptly reflected the personality of the dour new king, George V.

The revived image was rather more robust than that issued from 1887 with shorter and thicker sceptres between the fields. Many of these later coins survived in circulation until the early 1970s.

AU

EF showing wear to crown and lions

EF

Check the usual places for early wear such as the sceptres (especially at their inner ends), the lions' faces (but see previous page) and the crowns.

VF

There should still be a good amount of detail on the crowns, especially on the later series and the St. George's cross in the centre should still be recessed below the level of the surrounding garter.

F

Wear tends to be quite even, and although much detail has been lost, the basic design still stands out in bold relief.

Fair

The design is less clear and wear is beginning to encroach on the heraldic symbols within the shields. Thanks to the heavy rim, the legend and date should remain intact.

This was the last coin issued for circulation with this general style of reverse. It differed from its predecessors in the proportion of the legend which was now on the reverse, and having the crowns switched to the outer edge of the sceptres.

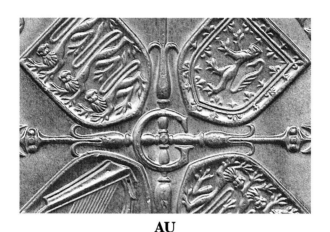

AU

EF. Slight but obvious wear on lower parts of shields and sceptres

EF

Wear is disconcertingly even, but in this example the centre of the coin has begun to wear around the 'G'

VF

Flattening is evident on the outer edges of the shields, the inner part of the sceptres and the crowns.

F

Grading here is just a question of degree – the fleurs de lys on the outer part of the Scottish shield are in the process of disappearing and the shields and crowns are much flatter than before.

Fair

The fleurs de lys at the top of the shield have now effectively gone and the harp and lions are merging with the shield edges.

Perhaps a little fussy, but a welcome change from the hackneyed cruciform shields that had graced the coinage from the days of Charles II and stumbled on in one form or another until 1960.

These coins tend to wear from the rim inwards, so it is not unusual to see a piece on which the shields are still quite clear, but the legend has been largely obliterated.

UNC

EF. Wear to sceptres and fleurs de lys

EF

In this coin, what little wear there is can best be seen on the sceptres which flank the crown and the date.

VF

Wear is quite general, but most detail has gone from the lions' faces, and there is a flattening of most parts of the design. The edges of the shields and the thistle will be noticeably worn.

F

Continuing much as before. Wear on the rim has not yet started to encroach and generally speaking all parts of the design are still fairly bold.

Fair

Edges of shields are worn more than in the previous photograph and the beading has now eroded completely taking with it the tops of some of the letters. Design and unusually, the motto are still intact.

Another attractive image in a generally well-liked series. Similar in many ways to the florin, but the shields are all set to the horizontal rather than being at an angle to one another.

A well struck example of this design in almost perfect condition

EF

There is plenty to grade here but in particular, the rose should have no more than just the slightest wear on its highest points – note however that the detail on the thistle is not as well defined as on many other coins . Shillings are a little small to show up much detail on the lions' faces, but imagine the ideal of the face coming towards a dome; any slight flattening is likely to be caused by wear. One further point to check here is that the tongue of the buckle stands proud of the frame – in lower grades the two components are likely to have merged.

EF

Very slight wear on the fleurs de lys. A useful clue is that in this grade, the tongue of the buckle should be distinct.

VF

The edges of the shields start to wear and there is likely to be some obvious erosion on the crowns, especially the fleurs de lys.

F

Crowns heavily worn and higher points can appear quite flat.

Fair

Despite considerable wear, the designs in the shields are still comparatively clear - this will in fact be one of the last places to completely erode.

Three shillings
Eighteen Pence

There are actually two closely related reverses here, the early type which has an oak wreath and was minted 1811-12, and the subsequent style in which the oak was supplemented with laurel.

EF

There is precious little to grade here, but the touchstones are the acorns and the laurel berries, much as they are in later designs.

VF

F

Shilling 1831-87
Sixpence 1831-1910

The oak and laurel wreath design was one of the more long lived images on British coinage, appearing in essentially the same form, at various points between 1831 and 1910.

UNC

EF

Look out for wear on the acorns and the outer edges of the oak leaves especially the large one at 3 o'clock. The jewels on the crown too should be checked under a magnifying glass for the beginnings of wear.

VF

The stones on the crown will be wearing, but at this stage should still be quite visible.

F
Crown becoming rather blurred but still some detail remaining.

Fair
Crown little more than an outline and most oak leaves completely flat.

Threepence 1834-1926
Twopence 1838-48
Three Halfpence 1834-70

The wreath and crown look more at home on these coins, where an intricate design would have lost much detail in the minting process. This simple design is in essence still used today in the special coins produced for the Royal Maundy.

There is not a lot to grade in isolation, just follow the pictures to chart the relative wear on the crown and wreath (which incidentally, is entirely of oak leaves whereas that on the sixpence and shilling is oak and laurel).

AU. Earlier crown (to 1887) showing an amazing amount of detail for a tiny coin

AU. Later crown

EF

The central stone can show most early wear but may not always be fully struck up.
The quality of strike can be quite poor, especially during the war years.

VF

F

Fair

Intended purely for circulation in Malta, the third-farthing was introduced in 1827 to replace a local denomination, the grano, which was valued at one twelfth of a penny. Surprisingly, considering its low value, it continued to be minted right up until the eve of the First World War. The earlier coins shared their designs with the British copper series of the time, but following the adoption of bronze for the lower value British denominations, the original third-farthing was replaced with an even smaller design, bearing a unique cut-down bun head on the obverse and a simple statement of value, oak wreath, date and crown on the reverse.

The bronze coins only bear nine dates during a period of issue amounting to 47 years, every year barring 1876 being issued to a strict monetary value i.e. £200 in 1866, £50 in 1868, £100 in 1913 etc., the total value of the entire bronze issue being slightly over £800.

The United Kingdom may have received some local kudos for maintaining a popular local coin, but judging by the condition of most survivors, the Maltese never actually got round to using them. It is for example almost unknown for coins issued in the two final years (1902 and 1913) to sink below VF.

The third-farthing was never made legal tender in the United Kingdom which rather sums up this strange little coin.

Practically as struck

EF

Little to actually grade bar the condition of the crown. It should be noted that standards of production and engraving were not that high (e.g. the extremely crude oak wreath), so check that what you think is wear, is not actually caused by other factors.

VF

Due mainly to their rarity (48,420 examples in a 9 year period), wreath crowns will always be sought after. Quite easy to grade if you follow the pictures; the most obvious points being the centre of the rose, the thistle and the stone under the cross. Most common in EF condition or thereabouts, with the lower grades being comparatively unusual.

The better coin here (top 2 images) is a proof in **FDC** condition. The standard of strike was generally very good, but even so this is no guarantee that all the detail on a 'business' strike will be fully struck up even in the best condition. The second coin is **EF.**

EF

The highest points of the roses and thistles will show just the slightest of flattening, as will the orb and the stones on the crown.

VF

Continuing as before but the individual stamen on the rose may not now be visible, and the higher points of the thistle will have rubbed off.

F

All high points have now flattened off to some extent, with little detail remaining in the rose centres.

Both these denominations were introduced for circulation in Ceylon, the half far-thing in 1828 and the quarter farthing (there were no less than 3840 to the pound!) in 1839. Initially the design of the half farthing followed the other copper coins of the period in having a Britannia reverse. From 1839 however, a simple crown, statement of value, date and rose/thistle/shamrock was substituted in its stead, a design which it shared with the quarter farthing.

From 1839 too, the larger coin became legal tender in the United Kingdom, and circulated, not entirely successfully for the next 30 years.

Both AU

EF

Wear is most evident on the thistle and rose, a fact which continues right down the grading scale.

VF

The fur on the lowest part of the crown now appears largely flat.

F

The rose is by now essentially flat and the outer stones on the upper part of the crown have disappeared.

Fair

The lettering is becoming faint and there is little or no detail on the rose, thistle and shamrock.

The wind of change blowing through Britain's coinage in the mid-1920s was, perhaps oddly, most felt in these two denominations. Gone were the well-used designs of yesteryear, to be replaced by the novel concept of three oak sprigs bearing respectively three and six acorns, so if you were unsure of the coin's value, you just counted the acorns! From a numismatic point of view, this was in its small way as much of a revolutionary step as Pistucci's George & Dragon or William Wyon's Gothic crowns and florins.

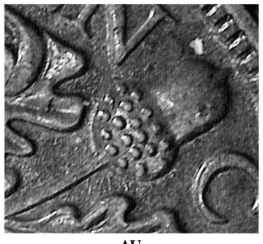

AU

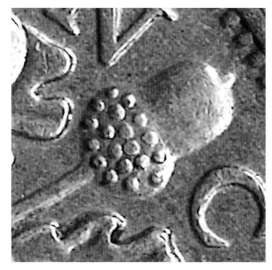

EF showing very slight wear on the acorn cup

EF

The best, in fact the only, way to grade these is with reference to the wear on the acorns and in this respect, it is not unlike grading a wreath crown. In EF condition, the detail (i.e. the pimples on the cup) should be clear and more or less round topped. Buy a decent magnifying glass to spot an AU…

VF

One or two of the higher pimples (there is probably a botanical term for these!) may be on the point of obliteration, but the vast majority will still be complete.

F
The higher points of the acorns are now flat, as are the higher points of the oak leaves.

Fair
No recognisable detail, the design just being a mere outline, but fortunately this is as bad as they get.

Something of a Plain Jane with very little on which to pass a grading judgement. Try the ball under the crown and the tops of the fleurs de lys, also the line at the bottom of the crown can register some wear. Best to follow the pictures, but other than that, just turn it over and look at the obverse!

AU

EF
The most obvious point of reference is the orb below the cross which may have picked up some slight wear. A magnifying glass is a must.

VF
The orb has now quite obviously flattened and some wear is evident on the fleurs de lys.

F

Holes through which the individual letters interlock begininning to fade away. Rim should also be distict from teeth in this grade.

Fair

Line at bottom of crown now broken by wear. Letters have merged together with no sign of an overlap.

The last silver 3d issued for general circulation, but the denomination exists in aspic as part of the Maundy set.

Because of their diminutive size, threepenny 'joeys' (a nickname also applied to the fourpence) were never very popular and eventually drifted out of circulation in the 1950s.

The final reverse design for these coins in circulation form, depicted the cross of St. George on a Tudor rose; a pleasant but hardly memorable design.

EF
Not a lot to go on, but the lettering should be sharp. The outermost parts of the rose can also pick up a little wear.

VF
Due to restricted circulation, few coins fall below this grade.

The sixpence was perforce re-designed as a result of Indian independence in August 1947. The earlier design of George VI had included the letter 'I' for Imperator or Emperor of India, a title which the king could no longer hold. The new design was simply a royal monogram, similar to that used on the pillar boxes of the time. Arguably though, the result was a marginal improvement on its predecessor.

EF

Check details on crown for early signs of wear.

VF
Orb and stones will now be showing obvious signs of wear.

F
Although there is, on the face of it, not a lot to go on, just check the loop where the two parts of the 'R' overlap, and that line at the bottom of the crown which is rapidly disappearing. You are however, unlikely to find a more worn specimen than this.

Taking its cue from the 1927-36 sixpence but with national unity as its theme (i.e. intertwined rose, thistle, shamrock and leek), this was an unusually intricate design.

Whilst the Gillick obverse could wear quite quickly, the multiple high points on the reverse seem to have protected this particular surface from too much erosion, and as a result, I have yet to see it reduced to worse than NVF.

The pick of the '1953-70 bunch'?

UNC. As good as a non-proof Elizabeth II sixpence gets

EF

Slight wear can occur almost anywhere, but as per usual the easiest point to check is the centre of the rose. This coin is rather weakly struck.

VF

Wear on the rose will not be as diagnostic as on the florin, and perhaps the most noticeable erosion comes on the side of the thistle. Not a grading exercise for beginners.

Introduced at the suggestion of slot machine manufacturers, the brass threepence represented another milestone in that it was the first British coin designed to be anything other than round*. It was at first produced alongside the silver threepence, but utterly replaced it in the fullness of time. Because of its small size, the silver threepence had never been very popular with the result that when the brass version appeared, it was welcomed by the public and remained a well-liked coin throughout its comparatively short life.

This is a simple design, with little to grade, but what there is is quite diagnostic, the touchstone being the thrift flower heads which range from three bold rings (i.e. flowers) per head in the top grades to some faint visual 'noise' in fair. The leaves of the plant are also worth investigating.

*Some of the siege pieces of the Civil War may be an exception, but in their case the word 'designed' would be something of an overstatement.

Detail of a brass threepence, practically as struck with full lustre

EF

EF

VF

F

Fair

A revival of the portcullis design used under the first Elizabeth, which itself picked up on a theme from the late Roman Empire. Another hard-wearing image which is seldom seen much below VF.

UNC

EF

Very difficult to distinguish from coins in the highest grades; what little wear there is, is likely to appear on the rivets at the angles of the portcullis. Occasionally a little erosion on the stone in the centre of the crown.

VF

As above, but wear is more pronounced.

To underline the maritime power of the United Kingdom, ships had featured on the reverse of British coins from the beginning of the modern period. However, this was the first time that the vessel, in this case a representation of Sir Francis Drake's *Golden Hind*, had taken centre stage.

UNC. This coin was only recently released from a mint roll but nevertheless has some slight scratches and imperfections on the highest points.

EF

The first signs of rubbing can appear almost anywhere, but specifically check out the crows' nests, the rigging and the flags at the mastheads.

VF

The crosses on the pennants, always rather faint, are beginning to disappear, as are the portholes just above the waterline. The edges of the sails are also beginning to show signs of wear.

F

The portholes have almost completely disappeared and the rigging has merged with the ship's side, which in turn is merging with the sea.

The humble farthing was completely re-designed as part of the abortive Edward VIII coinage, but most of the reverse designs re-appeared for 1937 with his brother, George VI on the obverse. It is easy to overlook what a revolutionary coin this was. Centuries of royal insignia, coats of arms and grandiose images of non-existent semi-deities had been replaced by a simple wild bird and a small and almost insignificant one at that. The design is unfussy, accurate and attractive.

Little needs to be said about the grading of these coins as they saw restricted circulation and seldom turn up in grades less than VF. Unless you have stumbled upon an extremely rare variety, anything grading below EF will be to all intents and purposes valueless. Not having any sharp edges to the design, what wear there is tends to be evenly distributed, although the wing tends to take a little more than its fair share of any rubbing.

FDC Toned. An evenly toned 1953 proof farthing

EF

VF

Many of the abbreviations used in this book are standard Coin collectors jargon, there are however, a few that may not be so obvious. This glossary should clear things up:

Alignment: The relationship between the obverse and reverse of the coin. Either the reverse is up-side-down compared to the obverse when rotated with fingers at the top and bottom of the coin, or the reverse is up the same way when the coin is rotated with fingers at the top and bottom of the coin. The latter is the most common alignment for British coins dated 1860-date and may be referred to as up/up. In the same way the upside down alignment may sometimes be referred to as up/down.

Berries: Usually refers to the number of berries in the wreath around the monarch's head. Or, in the case of reverses, usually the number of berries in the branch that Britannia holds.

BV: Bullion Value. i.e no collectors premium over the value of the metal.

EF: *Extremely Fine*: A grading term indicating a coin with little sign of being circulated. There may be only the slightest wear to the highest areas and minimal scratches and other marks. Often some of the mint lustre is visible on coins of this grade. As a rough idea a coin in your change would probably be an EF if it had been lucky and was minted just 1 year ago.

Exergue: The portion of a coin below the main design which usually houses the date.

Fair: A grading term indicating a heavily worn coin, but with readable legend and major points of design identifiable. It would be reasonable to say that the vast bulk of 20th century coins in this condition are worth no more than their metal value.

Fine: A grading term to indicate a coin that shows considerable wear to all raised surfaces. Some detail should be visible on the designs and some of the main hair volume should be visible on the Monarch's head. Not individual strands, but maybe a parting or signs of head-dress. Many of the coins in your pocket even after just 30 years or less of normal use would probably be Fine or lower.

H: An 'H' after the date in the first column indicates the coin was struck at the Heaton Mint in Birmingham. The 'H' mintmark will appear on the coin either next to, or under its date.

Inescutcheon: A smaller coat of arms entirely confined within the bounds of a larger one.

Incuse: Struck inwards. Lettering or a design element on a coin that is the opposite to raised. For example, the edge lettering on the modern £1 coin.

KN: A 'KN' after the date in the first column indicates the coin was struck at the Kings Norton Mint in Birmingham. The 'KN' will appear on the coin next to the date.

Modified Effigy: (George V only) In the absence of a direct comparison, the modified effigy (or modified head) can be distinguished by the initials which appear on the truncation of the neck. Before modification, the initials B.M. are placed near the centre of truncation. After modification they appear, without stops, well to the right thus: BM (not B.M.) The initials are those of the designer of the coin: Bertram Mackennal.

Mule: A Mule is when a coin gets made with the wrong combination of obverse and reverse.

Obverse: (or Obv) The side of the coin with the head of the Monarch on.

Pattern: A proposed coin type that was not used for circulation.

Piedfort: A coin that is struck on a thicker blank than is usual. Relatively recently the Royal mint starting coining Silver Piedfort coins.

Pointing/Points: To distinguish a different die used to strike a particular coin, often 'pointings' are used. They normally refer to a letter or design element on the coin, and to whether it points directly at, or between two border teeth or another element of the coin.

Poor: A grading term indicating a very worn coin. Not just a smooth disk but an identifiable coin. However, the list of shortcomings can be extensive, ranging from a few letters obliterated in the legend, to coins in which virtually the only detail visible is the date. A very few coins will still retain a value over and above the metal content, but they would need to be pretty rare.

Proof: A special striking of a coin using specially prepared and polished dies and blanks.

Reverse: (or Rev) The opposite side of the coin to the obverse, or the 'tails' side.

Teeth/Beads: The small teeth or circles surrounding the inner rim of many British coins. Beads are circular, teeth are elongated.

Truncation: (or trunc) The base of the monarch's neck, often containing the designers initials.

UNC: *Uncirculated.* A grading term indicating a coin, which like the name suggests, should be as it left the mint with no signs of circulation or wear. Not necessarily perfect though, because coins can pick up scratches and what are known as 'bag marks' during mass production and contact with other coins at the mint. The coin should have most of its lustre present and some dealers may expect 100% lustre on coins stated as Uncirculated.

VF: *Very Fine.* A grading term describing a coin with some wear to the highest areas of the design but which has seen limited circulation. More hair detail is evident and also detail on the other designs. Just as an average guide a coin that has been in normal circulation for approximately 5 years may qualify for VF status.

In a project as large as this, it goes without saying that I relied on both dealers and private individuals to supply me with coins and photographs of coins in the range of conditions that I required. I am therefore heavily indebted to the following:

Chris Perkins at Predecimal.com (www.predecimal.com)
Michael Gouby at Michael Coins (www.michael-coins.co.uk)
Susan Smith at Ye Olde Banknote Shoppe (www.oldbanknoteshop.co.uk)
Colin Goode (www.aboutfarthings.co.uk)
Graeme Monk (www.croydoncoinauctions.co.uk)
Rob Pearce (www.rpcoins.co.uk)
Dave Webb at OneWebby International (www.onewebby.com)
David Stuart at Alnwick British & Colonial Coins & Tokens
(www.abccoinsandtokens.com)
Dave Allen at Cambridge Coins & Jewellery (www.cambridgecoins.co.uk)
Jonathan Cavendish at Cavendish Collectables (www.cavendish-collectables.co.uk)
Andy & Neelam Bruce (www.onlinecoins.co.uk)
Stephen Clarke at Daluka Coins & Collectables

Colin Adams, Ken Burns, Barry Clack, Gareth Davies, Charlie Gooda, Lance Hartland, David T. Hughes, Peter Ireland, Clive King, Philip Lloyd, Ian Lovett, Livio Martinkovic, Duncan McKinnon, Terry Page, Martin Platt, Lloyd Roberts, Paul Robinson, Polishchuk Sergey, Rebecca Sheen, Alan Smith, Richard Stoker, Rob Stringfellow, Julie Sutton, Malcolm Taylor, Dene Venter, John Williams, Mark Yandell

Also sincere thanks to Bob Crawford for his assistance with the Sheldon Scale.

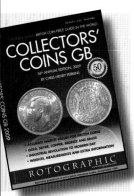

This book was published by
Rotographic International.

First Edition - 2009

www.rotographic.com

PO Box 49432
London, SE20 7ZJ

0871 871 5122.